Dedicated to my loving mother and father,

who taught me a deep appreciation of the

beauty and healing power of nature.

Pussy Willows *for* Windolyn

by Lucy Shepard

Illustrated by T.LAk

It was a late winter's day in New England.
And the air was filled with the sweet smell
of the coming season. Robins had arrived
singing about the promise of spring, and
the rebirth of nature.

The farmer trudged through the snow covered field. He walked with a pep in his step this early March day. He was in search of the first flowers of spring...Pussy willows.

The rain left streaks of water dripping down the window pane of Room 34. The room was alive with anticipation. Their teacher would be introducing a promised activity on this special day.
"Is it time for our special art project?" was the cry.

For every year on this day, the Room 34 students had created a bulletin board of drawings for the approaching spring season.

RM 34
SPRIN
PROJECT

The farmer had reached an area known as the run.
For a moment, maybe two, he gazed up and pondered
where he was standing. Within his view was the
boulder which marked the 300 year old location of the
first family cabin.

Charlie continued his search. To his delight, he spied a bush full of newly blossomed pussy willows. He gently clipped a few branches. With his fingers, he brushed over the blossoms and smelled their rich, earthy aroma.

The first grade classroom buzzed with excitement as the children gathered on the carpeted floor. They giggled as the pussy willow branches passed through their small fingers. Their senses alive with each touch and smell of the soft, gray colored buds with that aroma of the outdoors.

Drawing materials of paint, crayons, and construction paper lay on the tables before them. Templates for vases, wallpaper scraps and paste awaited their creativity.

GLUE

With the precious flowers in hand, the farmer
walked back through the field to the
farmhouse. The sun had begun to set.

10.

Once inside, he quickly found twine and tied the flowers into a neat bundle. His fingers finished the finicky bouquet with a bow.

He made his way out to the car and carefully placed the bundle on the seat. He admired the package on the seat every once in a while as he drove down to the local hospital to visit his wife.

The teacher gathered her students as she demonstrated some techniques of dipping a finger to dab the gray and brown paint on paper to recreate the blossoms that were in view.

All the children were now engaged, drawing long brown branches with their tiny fingers, along with dabs of gray for buds haphazardly placed in random places on each paper.

Others took to cutting and pasting pieces of paper
to create wallpaper vases. Paste, paper, and paint
was everywhere much to the chagrin
of their teacher.

Charlie parked his car in the hospital's visitors lot and carefully lifted the bundle from the seat. At the front desk, he asked for his wife's room number. The nurse escorted him to Lois' brightly lit room.

Lovingly, Charlie gently placed the bouquet
of freshly clipped pussy willows at her side.

Lois presented to her husband
their newborn daughter.

17.

As she drove home from another long and busy day at school, smiled as she thought about her day with her students. Of all the art projects she created with her children, this was a favorite.

Many warm memories flooded her mind of past birthdays. She parked her car and hurried into the house past rain drops that still lingered from earlier in the day. Shaking off the chill she unlocked the sunroom door.

Displayed in a vase was a bouquet
of fresh cut pussy willows. She
opened the envelope and smiled at
the birthday card inside.

The card read:
"Happy Birthday Windolyn...
Another year of pussy willows for you."

Love, Mom and Dad.

The END